Ulysse A. DAA-KPODE
Zoul-kifouli ADEOTI

Genetic diversity of dessert and plantain banana varieties

Ulysse A. DAA-KPODE
Zoul-kifouli ADEOTI

Genetic diversity of dessert and plantain banana varieties

Genetic variability of dessert banana and plantain varieties grown in Central and Southern Benin

ScienciaScripts

Imprint

Any brand names and product names mentioned in this book are subject to trademark, brand or patent protection and are trademarks or registered trademarks of their respective holders. The use of brand names, product names, common names, trade names, product descriptions etc. even without a particular marking in this work is in no way to be construed to mean that such names may be regarded as unrestricted in respect of trademark and brand protection legislation and could thus be used by anyone.

Cover image: www.ingimage.com

This book is a translation from the original published under ISBN 978-620-2-54084-1.

Publisher:
Sciencia Scripts
is a trademark of
International Book Market Service Ltd., member of OmniScriptum Publishing Group
17 Meldrum Street, Beau Bassin 71504, Mauritius
Printed at: see last page
ISBN: 978-620-2-93719-1

INTRODUCTION

INTRODUCTION

The *Musa Spp* banana tree is one of the most important crops in the world. It is native to Southeast Asia (BAKRY) *et al.*, 2002)and is grown in more than 120 countries in the intertropical zones (Jones, 2000). It belongs to the class of Monocotyledons, of the order *Zingiberals* and to the family Musaceae. There are two genera: the genus Musa and the genus Ensete (Champion, 1963). The most cultivated banana species belong to the Musa genus. These are essentially *Musa accuminata* and *Musa balbisiana* (BAKRY *et al.*, 2002). These two species are at the origin of the various cultivars classified on the basis of their morphological characteristics and genetic make-up. There are currently more than 500 varieties of edible banana trees (Perrier and Montcel, 1990). From a culinary point of view, there are 2 types of bananas: dessert bananas and cooking bananas or plantains. Bananas and plantains are a vital food resource for more than 400 million people in inter-tropical areas (Lassois, Busogoro et Jijakli, 2009)and contribute to food security because of their high energy (carbohydrates) and nutritional value (rich in minerals and vitamins in particular) (Jones, 2000). They also contribute to local and regional economic development by guaranteeing regular income to producers because of their continuous production throughout the year (Odah *et al.*, 2013). The banana is the most exported fruit in the world with 18 million tonnes per year (ODEADOM, 2012).

In Benin, fruit production is booming and is estimated at around 2,500 tonnes in 2009 (Tossou, Floquet et Sinsin, 2012)in the Allada plateau in South Benin. At that time, bananas took fifth place after pineapple, orange, mandarin, and mango with an estimated annual production of 29 tons in the same area, the largest growing region. Unfortunately, for several years in Benin, the banana tree was relegated to the background of fruit crops to be promoted, which justifies the almost inexistence of statistical data at the national level on its production. Indeed, national production is intended for the local market, and remains insufficient to cover demand (Lokossou et Achigan, 2000). Little research has been devoted to the banana tree in Benin. The varieties of bananas cultivated are still very little known and their genetic diversity is unknown. Knowledge of the level of diversity of a species and its structure enables the best conservation strategies to be defined on the one hand, and varietal improvement on the other. To do this, molecular markers appear to be better tools for assessing plant diversity. Moreover, genetic characterisation is also the starting point for any programme of promotion and varietal improvement.

This work will contribute to improving knowledge of the varietal diversity of cultivated banana trees. In Benin, this study will be the starting point for future research work on the characterisation of banana trees. The general objective is to assess the genetic diversity of dessert and plantain banana trees using microsatellite molecular markers. Specifically, this involved :

- Determine the level of genetic diversity within dessert and plantain bananas
- Determine the structuring of this diversity according to the areas of culture
- Clarify the problems of synonymy and homonymy of vernacular names.

This document is structured in three main parts. After the introduction, the first part is devoted to a synthesis of previous work on the different aspects addressed in this study. The second part presents the framework, study material and methods used. In the third part, we have proceeded with the presentation of our findings and discussion. Finally, the conclusion and perspectives are presented.

CHAPTER I: BIBLIOGRAPHICAL REVIEW

1- GENERAL INFORMATION ON BANANAS

1.1 Origin

The banana tree native to Southeast Asia is currently cultivated in many parts of the world, mainly in Latin America and Vuylsteke, 2001)Africa (Swennen and Vuylsteke, 2001). The first traces of the banana tree found in India are fossils from the Tertiary era. The banana tree (*Musa spp*) is probably one of the first plants domesticated in Asia, and later spread to the Pacific. It was introduced to Africa, first around 1000 BC and then in the 5th century AD. The wild diploid species *Musa acuminata* Colla (genome AA) and *Musa balbisiana* Colla (genome BB) are at the origin of most of the banana trees cultivated today. These two species are very fertile and can reproduce by seed (sexual) and by rejection (vegetative) (Golden and Varoquaux, 2006).

1.2 Systematics of the banana tree

Banana trees are monocotyledons of the order Scitaminales or Zingiberals belonging to the family *Musaceae* (Simmonds, 1966). This family comprises three genera: *Musella*, *Ensete* and *Musa*, with high variability and five sections *Eumusa*, *Rhodochlamys*, *Callimusa*, *Australimusa* and *Ingetimusa* (Simmonds, 1966). The first four sections belong to the genus *Musa* on the basis of the number of chromosomes and morphological characteristics (Lassoudière, 2010). Of the different sections, only the *Eumusa* section (n=11) yielded parthenocarpic species. This section includes 10 species. The two main species in this section are *Musa acuminata* (AA) and *Musa balbisiana* (BB). The haploid contribution of *M. acuminata* and *M. balbisiana* to bananas is indicated by A and B respectively (Simmonds and Shepherd, 1955; Lassois, Busogoro et Jijakli, 2009). *M. acuminata* is at the origin of all parthenocarpic banana trees, alone or with the participation of *M. balbisiana* (Lasssoudière, 2007). From a botanical point of view, the genus *Musa is* divided into two main types: inedible and edible varieties. The species with inedible or wild fruits can be used for other purposes such as fibre production and livestock feed (Lasssoudière, 2007). These species, all diploid (AA and BB), are often used in plant breeding for their disease resistance and fertility. Currently there are about 1800 varieties, all of which originate in Southeast Asia (Lassois *et al;* 2009). Edible varieties with fleshy fruits and without seeds number about 1 200. These varieties are divided into five groups according to their ploidy level and constitution: diploid groups AA and AB, triploid groups AAA, comprising the majority of fruit cultivars for export, including the subgroups Gros Michel, Cavendish, Yangambi Km 5 and AAB (Sivirihauma, 2013). They are essentially made up of cooking bananas with a predominance of plantains

(Photo 1) and ABB, comprising rustic banana trees yielding fruit to be eaten cooked (Lasssoudière, 2007). Among the banana trees, plantains constitute a fairly homogeneous group. They are all triploid ABB (Swennen, 1990). Several characters are used to distinguish plantains from other triploid AAB banana trees such as Pisang Awak, Pisang Kilat, Silk or pome: They have compound tepals, of a typical yellow-orange colour (Sivirihauma, 2013). Their male axis is usually absent, and when present it is covered with persistent bracts and remains of male flowers. They have long fruits with pinkish flesh which is very tasty when the fruit is ripe and has an unpleasant taste when the fruit is unripe (De Langhe, 1961). The species in the *Callimusa* (as *Musa coccinea*) and *Rhodoclamis* (as *Musa ornata*) sections are mainly of ornamental importance. As for the individuals of the *Australimusa* section, of which *Musa textilis* is the main representative, they are used in the manufacture of ropes for the navy and fishing industry (INIBAP, 2001).

Photo 1: Plantain banana harvested

1.3 Morphology of the plant

The banana tree is a giant grass that can grow to a height of 10 to 15 m (Simmonds, 1956). The pseudo-trunk is formed by the interlocking of the leaf sheaths. The leaves are emitted by the terminal meristem of the true underground stem called "bulb" (Lassois, Busogoro et Jijakli, 2009). This subterranean stem is the vital centre of the banana tree, the hub of the plant's development and of all nutritional exchanges. It is the place where the roots, leaves and inflorescence are formed (Lasssoudière, 2007). A schematic representation of the banana tree can be found in (figure 1).

Banana leaves consist of a sheath, a petiole and a blade with parallel secondary veins. The new leaves unfurl at the top of the pseudo-trunk. By convention, they are numbered from youngest to oldest (Bakry *et al*; 1997). A new leaf is formed every 7 to 10 days, although this period is extended when growing conditions are not optimal. The number of leaves varies according to cultivar and environmental conditions (Jones, 2000). A banana plant bears about 10-15 functional leaves at the time of inflorescence emergence (Lasssoudière, 2007).

The part of the inflorescence bearing the hands of female flowers, i.e. bananas, is called the bunch (figure 1): the ovaries develop into parthenocarpic fruits for the cultivated varieties (Lassoudière, 2010).

The harvested product, the banana, a few dozen of which are gathered in a bunch, is a berry, an indiscriminate fruit, asperm. This absence of seeds is due to the sterility of the cultivated varieties which results from genetic factors (reworking of chromosome segments, inter specificity) and triploidy (Doré et Varoquaux, 2006).

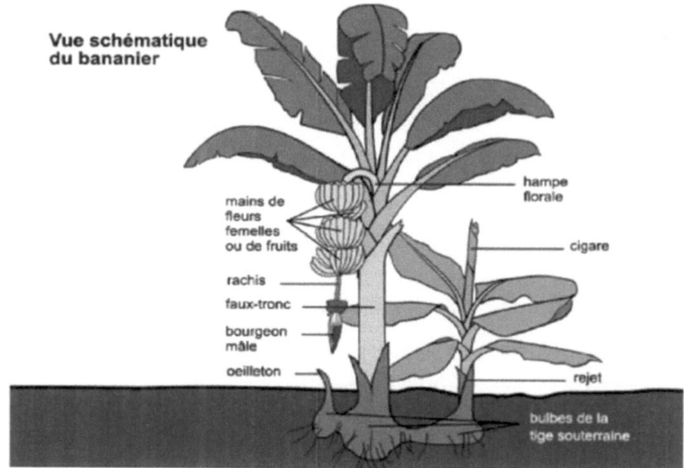

Figure 1*: Schematic view of a banana tree at its fruiting stage and its shoots according to Champion (1967).*

1.4 Ploidy level

The number of basic chromosomes in banana trees of the *Eumusa* section is n=x=11. A variety can be diploid (2n=2x=22), triploid (2n=3x=33) or tetraploid (2n=4x=44). Triploid cultivars are the most numerous and tetraploids are rare (Simmonds, 1962)(Simmonds, 1962). Chromosome counts, flow cytometry (Doležel) et Bartoš, 2005)and cytogenetic studies have made it possible to determine the level of ploidy of the cultivated banana varieties. Today, cultivated varieties are classified into groups according to their genetic make-up and ploidy level (Cirad- Flhor, 2003). While all wild banana trees are diploid, the varieties currently cultivated are generally sterile, aspermic triploid clones (AAB and ABB), resulting either from interspecific crosses between the two main diploid wild seminiferous species Musa acuminata and Musa balbisiana, or from the single species M. acuminata (AAA). Diploid varieties (AA and AB) and tetraploid clones of an interspecific nature are more rarely found (Lasssoudière, 2007). The haploid contribution of M. acuminata and M. balbisiana to cultivated bananas is indicated by A and B respectively (Simmonds et Shepherd, 1955). Within cultivated banana trees, a distinction must be made between two main types of edible bananas: bananas that are eaten fresh, known as "dessert", and bananas that are eaten cooked, known as "to be cooked", including plantains. The latter (AAB) include numerous cultivars that vary in shape, size, colour, taste, etc., and are used in a variety of ways.

1.5 Distribution in Benin

For a long time, banana production received very little attention at the level of state services, to the point where there are almost no statistics (surface area, production, yield) on the subject. However, survey and estimation work by Pedro (1999) indicated that in 1997, banana production was 22199 tonnes, representing 0.6% of total food production. In 1998, this production was 31050 tonnes. In 1999, it was estimated at 40,000 tonnes. The cultivation of banana and plantain trees is concentrated in the southern part of the country in the departments of Atlantique, Ouémé, Mono and Zou-sud. The total area occupied by banana and plantain trees is 20070 ha (Lokossou et Achigan, 2000).

1.6 Diversity in Benin

In Benin there are several varieties of dessert banana and plantain (Table 1) (Pédro, 1999). The vernacular **"sotounmon"** is a soft banana with a yellow skin when ripe (Photo 2) and is found almost everywhere. It is used to make doughnuts, cakes and local drinks. It is a banana that is available in all seasons but is very susceptible to disease and insects. The **"doheze"** banana with a green ripe skin is very popular for dessert because of its aroma. It can be found at the beginning of the rainy season. The **"dankoekoe"** is a soft banana with purple skin when ripe (Photo 3) which is often used during Vodoun ceremonies and also consumed as a dessert. Apart from the varieties mentioned, we also have sweet bananas such as **tchon, limu, gunkoekoe, sokoekoe, gbogui, hlo,** which are slightly acidic bananas that are also sought after on the market. They are a second option if SOTOUNMON and DOHEZE are rare.

It should be noted that the names attributed to sweet and plantain bananas are numerous and depend on the ethnic groups in the production areas. As for plantains, there is a whole range. The most important are the following: False horn **"aloga"** in the vernacular language, much sought-after for the manufacture of crisps, chips and fries. We find this variety of plantain on the market after the great rainy season: the True Horn variety: **"adjinakou"**, big plantain, grown on the top of the slopes. **awonlinkoekoe** (banana from Nigeria), **assonwonnou, gnivlan,** come after the others. These varieties are found during the rainy season. However, there are other varieties whose characteristics and vernacular names are not known. These are: Chinese banana, plantain banana, big michel and *Musa sinensis*. (Gbahoun, 1993). The cultivation of these various varieties is carried out around the huts and in small batches scattered throughout the fields. In recent years, banana production has been increasing, which has led to a significant increase in the area under cultivation, especially in the south of the country. In most banana plantations, a mixture of many varieties can be found on the same plot of land.

Table 1: Some vernacular names of bananas and plantains in Benin

PRODUCTS	VERNACULAR NAMES
dessert bananas	sotounmon, planta; dankoekoe,gbakoekoe; tchon, limu, gunkoekoe; sokoekoe, gbogui, doheze
plantains	adjinakou, assonwonnou; aloga,gnivlan, kpahissa; awonlin - koekoe; akpahissi; adjangan; aïvlan ;

Source: Pedro 1999; Adeoti et al.2016

Photo 2: Sotoumon

Photo 3: Dankoékoé

1.7 Cultivation systems

Several cropping systems are observed for bananas. Bananas are cultivated alone or in association with others, which is the most widespread cultivation system. Banana crops are also observed around huts or dwellings (Pedro, 1999; Adeoti et *al,* 2016). In most departments banana cultivation is associated with maize, cassava, cowpea and several other market garden products. The latter trend is also observed in the large urban areas, mainly at the level of market gardening sites. Pure banana cultivation is still very little developed or even non-existent (Adeoti et al.2016).

1.8 Importance of culture

1.8.1   Economic importance

Bananas are the fourth most important agricultural product in terms of world production after rice, wheat and maize. It ranks first in fruit production, with just over 117 million tonnes produced annually worldwide (Ganry *et al.*, 2012). It is cultivated in more than 120 countries on the 5 continents and on more than 10 million hectares (Bakry *et al.* 1997; Lassoudière 2007; Lassois *et al.* 2009). Nearly 90% of production comes from small farmers, producing for domestic consumption and local markets. Only 10% of global production is for export (Lassois, Busogoro et Jijakli, 2009). Bananas for cooking account for 43% of world production. Dessert bananas account for 57% of world production, with the majority coming from the Cavendish group. India is the largest producer, followed by Ecuador, China, Colombia and Costa Rica (Lassoudière, 2007). Other parts of the plant are used as a textile fibre, for shelter construction, blanket manufacture or as cooking packaging. The use of banana leaves as packaging in the commercial circuit of chikwanges and the use of leaves in the roofs of houses and stables, curtains, etc. are other economic aspects of the banana tree in the study area (Katungu, 2011).

1.8.2   Nutritional importance

The banana is above all a food plant cultivated for its fruit eaten fresh (dessert banana) or cooked (plantain and cooking banana), which are an important source of carbohydrates; it is a high-energy fruit. Bananas are rich in carbohydrates (22%), including glucose (20%), sucrose (65%) and fructose (15%). The protein (1.0%) and fat (0.5%) contents are insignificant. Bananas provide almost double the energy provided by apples and three times that of citrus fruits. It is rich in potassium but low in calcium, iron and sodium. It is a good source of vitamins A, B and C (Lasssoudière, 2007).

1.8.3   Agronomic importance

After harvesting, the pseudo-trunk and leaves of the banana tree produce good quality compost and serve as mulch (generic term for a layer formed by one or more elements on the soil surface). Banana sheaths are used in nurseries where suitable bags are not available and are particularly effective. The pseudo-trunk is used as logs in nurseries. In soil conservation, banana trees planted on contour lines retain runoff water and thus control water erosion (Sivirihauma, 2013).

1.8.4   Cultural importance

The banana tree produces by-products for non-food use, some of which are used in the manufacture of varied and pleasant art objects. These products are of cultural importance if they are exhibited in museums as art objects with interlacing dressed in sheaths of various colours; they make excellent ceilings in houses, curtains, baskets and "Mirago" or mats with an attractive appearance (Kanyaruguru, 1999).

1.8.5   Social importance

The banana tree plays an important role in people's culture. In the Great Lakes region in general, the banana tree materialises the presence of human society (Lassoudière, 2010). In Benin, it is used in customary ceremonies, and serves as an offering for deities (Lokossou and Achigan, 2000). Plantain bananas are much more often used as a present (gift) to offer to friends or for any other reason (Pédro, 1999).

1.8.6   Uses

Bananas are often eaten fresh. However, a number of by-products result from its processing and consumption patterns vary from country to country and sometimes from region to region within a country. Indeed, some varieties are consumed boiled, roasted (Photo 4) or fried (INFOCOMM, 2016). In addition to these commonly encountered modes of consumption, bananas are also used for the production of traditional beer (Simone, 1988). The pulp, which is dried and then reduced to flour, is used in the formulation of children's food (Lokossou et Achigan, 2000). In addition, banana leaves are used as food packaging and in the treatment of certain diseases (Lokossou, 1988). et Achigan, 2000; Adéoti *et al.*, 2016)

Photo 4: Grilled banana

2. Molecular markers

Molecular markers are defined as differences at the genotypic (DNA) level and can be used to explain genetic phenomena (Okogbenin and Fregene, 2003; Lokko *et al.*, 2005). To be useful as a genetic marker, the locus of the marker must show an experimentally detectable variation between individuals (Castelblanco et Fregene, 2006; Sørensen *et al.*, 2008). The variation may be due to single nucleotide polymorphisms or deletions/insertions, or large chromosomal changes. They can also be used for genome mapping, identifying the regions of the genome that control a trait and following a sequence of interest in a plant breeding programme (Ellis, 1994; Liu, 1998; Yan *et al.*, 2005; Okogbenin, Marin and Fregene, 2008). The level of polymorphism maintained at any locus in natural populations is determined by many factors including population size, mating or breeding habits, selection, mutation and migration rates (Tan ksley, 1994; Dettori, Quarta et Verde, 2001; Fregene *et al.*, 2003; Xia *et al.*, 2005). There are several types of molecular markers: enzyme markers, dominant markers and codominant markers. Among these, codominant markers appear to be the most discriminating and the most widely used today in genetic diversity studies.

2.1 Dominant markers

The dominant markers are genetic markers that reveal mass homozygosity in the population. That is, one of the alleles of a gene outweighs one of the two extreme variants of a phenotype or genotype. Some of the most commonly used dominant molecular markers include the following:

- **RAPD** (Random Amplified Polymorphic DNA), which consists of carrying out a PCR using a short primer of about ten nucleotides, with an arbitrary sequence. It requires a small quantity of DNA. It is a less expensive technique. But it has a low reproducibility.

- **AFLP** (Amplification Fragment Length Polymorphism). This technique is based on the joint detection of restriction site polymorphism and hybridization polymorphism of a primer of arbitrary sequence. It allows a quick and easy creation of genetic maps with accurate data and good reproducibility. But it is very expensive with variable discriminating power. It does not differentiate between homozygotes and heterozygotes.

2.2 Codominant markers

Codominant markers reveal in each individual in a population two or more different variants of a gene, known as alleles, which together participate in the determination of a particular trait, whether phenotypic or genotypic. There are several codominant molecular markers, of which the most widely used in genetic diversity are :

- **RFLP** (Restriction Fragment Length Polymorphism). It is a technique adapted to the construction of genetic linkage maps. It is inexpensive and highly reproducible with good stability. But it has a low level of polymorphism in some species and requires a lot of time and a large amount of DNA.

- Microsatellites (**SSR**) These are small, highly variable, repeated DNA sequences that can be used as indicative markers for genetic analysis.

2.3 Microsatellites (SSR)

Microsatellites reflect polymorphism (Figure 2) based on the number of repeat units (Weber et May, 1989; Akinbo, 2008). They are highly variable DNA sequences that can be used as indicative markers for genetic analysis. The number and composition of microsatellite repeats differ between plants. The frequency of repeats longer than 20 bp is estimated to occur every 33 kbp in plants (Agre, 2015). The most common forms of repetition are simple repetitions of di-nucleotides such as (CA) n, (GT) n, (GA) n: (CT) n, (CG) n: (GC) n and (AT) n: (TA) n, where n is the number of repetitions (Agre, 2015).

The SRS technique is based on PCR amplification of genomic DNA using specific primers flanking the repeated sequences. SSRs have proven to be very useful molecular markers in marker-assisted selection, analysis of genetic diversity of populations in several species (Gupta et Rustgi, 2004). They have been used in the study of diversity in several plants: in cassava (Agre, 2015); in millet (Adéoti*et al.*, 2017); in banana *Musa spp* (Onildo Nunes et al 2013; Irish *et al.*, 2014;)Singh, Sorokhaibam, etc.); in et Shrivastava, 2014)millet (Adéoti); and in *et al.*, 2017)banana *Musa spp* (Onildo Nunes et al 2013; Irish *et al.*, 2014;)Singh,

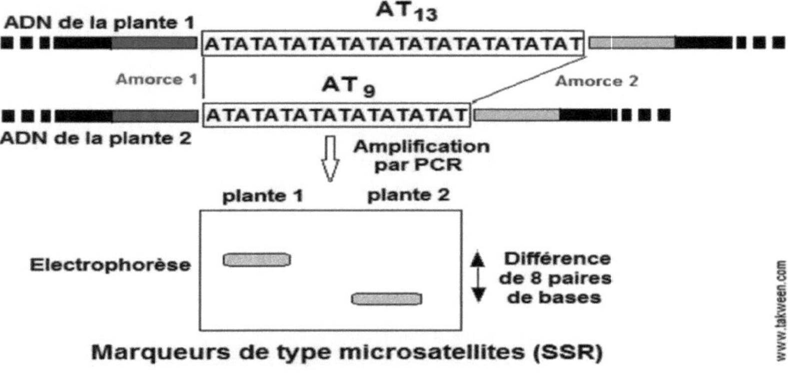

Sorokhaibam, etc.). et Shrivastava, 2014)

Figure 2: *Microsatellite marker www.biotech-ecolo.net/diversite-genetique-mesures/marqueurs-moleculaires-PCR.html accessed on 11-02-2018*

CHAPTER II: - METHODOLOGY

1. STUDY AREA

The accessions, which are the subject of a diversity study, were taken during previous collection missions and placed in collection at the Sékou experimental site. The collection areas cover central and southern Benin, representing five (05) departments (Table 2; Figure 3).

Table 2: Origins of the different accessions characterised

N°	Department	Region
1	Hill	Centre
2	Mono	South
3	Couffo	South
4	Zou	Centre
5	Atlantic	South

Figure 3*: Geographical distribution of prospected sites*

2. WORKING ENVIRONMENT

The different manipulations in the context of the realisation of this dissertation were carried out at the Laboratory of Microbiology and Food Technologies (LAMITA) of the UAC. Although it is a microbiology laboratory, LAMITA has a technical platform for genotyping. LAMITA is located on the premises of the Institute of Applied Biomedical Sciences (ISBA) at the FSS (Faculty of Science and Health) at the fairgrounds.

3. MATERIALS AND METHODS

3.1 Plant material

The plant material consists of different varieties of dessert and plantain banana trees. Ninety-four (94) samples were taken from the collection installed on the experimental site of the Faculty of Agricultural Sciences in Sékou. The samples consisted of 59 accessions (Table 3) of dessert bananas and 35 (Table 4) accessions of plantain.

Table 3: List of characterised dessert banana accessions

Sample No.	Name Vernaculars	Department	Region
1	Sotoumon	Atlantic	South
2	Abalayé	Atlantic	South
3	Agbavlan	Mono-Couffo	south
4	Agbodjouba	Atlantic	South
5	Agbodjouba	Atlantic	South
6	Agbola Koladé	zou-colline	centre
7	Akaléda	zou-colline	centre
8	Akokoé	zou-colline	centre
9	Allokpé	Mono-Couffo	south
10	Amahoui	Atlantic	South
11	Amanwi	Atlantic	South
12	Anon Gblè-lè	Atlantic	South
13	Anon Gblè-lè	Mono-Couffo	south
14	Atchanfan	Atlantic	South
15	Atchoin	Atlantic	South
16	Chinese	Atlantic	South
17	Collette	zou-colline	centre
18	Dan Kôdou	Mono-Couffo	south
19	Dan kokoe	Atlantic	South
20	Dan Mandan	Mono-Couffo	south
21	Dan Yotchio	Mono-Couffo	south
22	Danvlan	Mono-Couffo	south
23	Djanglè	zou-colline	centre
24	Djigba Kokoé	zou-colline	centre
25	Dohèzè	Atlantic	South
26	Edan Mandan	Mono-Couffo	south
27	Edô Mandan	Mono-Couffo	south

28	Ehoun Mandan	Mono-Couffo	south
29	Fanoukolè	zou-colline	centre
30	Gbakokoé	Atlantic	South
31	Gbakokoé	Atlantic	South
32	Chinese Gbakokoe	Mono-Couffo	south
33	Gnimangnan	Mono-Couffo	south
34	Kinkou	Atlantic	South
35	Kôdou	Mono-Couffo	south
36	Kotchoukpoui	Mono-Couffo	south
37	Kpafoutou	Atlantic	South
38	Lêkê	Atlantic	South
39	Limou	Mono-Couffo	south
40	Ma kokoé	Mono-Couffo	south
41	Oguédé Adjatchè	zou-colline	centre
42	Oguèdè Atacora	zou-colline	centre
43	Oguédé Cotonou	Atlantic	South
44	Oguèdè Ghana	zou-colline	centre
45	Oguédé Ognibo (dwarf)	zou-colline	centre
46	Ominin Adjatchè	zou-colline	centre
47	Ominin Gambari	zou-colline	centre
48	Pantifou	Atlantic	South
49	Planta	Atlantic	South
50	Planta	Mono-Couffo	south
51	Planta	Mono-Couffo	south
52	Sotoumon	Mono-Couffo	south
53	Sotoumon	Mono-Couffo	south
54	Sotoumon	Mono-Couffo	south
55	Sotoumon	Mono-Couffo	south
56	Tchon	Atlantic	South
57	Tokpovi	Mono-Couffo	south
58	Wontissu	Mono-Couffo	south
59	Wontissu	Mono-Couffo	south

Table 4: List of characterised plantain accessions

Sample No.	Vernacular Names	Department	Region
1	Alloga Kô Awé	Atlantic	south
2	Adjagan Ayavlan	Mono-Couffo	south
3	Adjagan kô Awé	Mono-Couffo	south

4	Adjangan	Mono-Couffo	south
5	Adjangan	Mono-Couffo	south
6	Adjangan Ayawé	Mono-Couffo	south
7	Adjangan Ayawé	Mono-Couffo	south
8	Adjangan Kô Awé	Mono-Couffo	south
9	Adjangan Akpahissi	Mono-Couffo	south
10	Agbaagba	Mono-Couffo	south
11	Agbaagba Vôvô	zou-colline	centre
12	Agnivlan	Atlantic	south
13	Akpaziwé	zou-colline	centre
14	Alloga	Mono-Couffo	south
15	Alloga Kô Aton	zou-colline	centre
16	Alloga Ko ènin	zou-colline	centre
17	Alloga Wéwé	Atlantic	south
18	Alloga Vôvô	Atlantic	south
19	Alloga Vôvô	zou-colline	centre
20	Alloga Vôvô	Mono-Couffo	south
21	Alloga Kô Awé	Atlantic	south
22	Alloga Kpahissi	zou-colline	centre
23	Alloga	Atlantic	south
24	Avlan Djangan	Mono-Couffo	south
25	Avlô Kpahissi	Atlantic	south
26	Djangan	Mono-Couffo	south
27	Djangan Kô Awé	Mono-Couffo	south
28	Unknown	zou-colline	south
29	Kpahissi	Atlantic	south
30	Mandangan	Mono-Couffo	south
31	Mandangan	Mono-Couffo	south
32	Mandangan	Mono-Couffo	south
33	Mandangan Kô Awé	Mono-Couffo	south
34	Mandangan Dékpo	Mono-Couffo	south
35	Mandangan Kpahouitchi	Mono-Couffo	south

3.2 Genotyping

3.2.1   DNA extraction

The extraction of DNA from the samples was done according to the protocol routinely used in the laboratory using MATAB (Mixed Alkyl Trimethyl Ammonium Bromide) as the lysis buffer. Approximately 100mg of fresh banana leaves were ground in a mortar with 700 µl of MATAB extraction buffer (100 mM Tris-HCl, 1.4 M NaCl, 20 mM EDTA, 2% MATAB, 1% PEG 6000, 0.5% sodium sulphite, and pH 8) boiled at 65°C. The mixture was poured into an Eppendorf tube and then heated for 40 minutes at 65°C in a bain Marie. Then 500µl of Chloroform Isoamyl Alcohol 24:1 was added to the mixture to remove plant debris and trap DNA and centrifuged at 13,000 rpm for 10 minutes. The supernatant was transferred to a new, carefully labelled Eppendorf tube. This chloroform washing step was repeated a second time to remove as much plant debris as possible. To the recovered supernatant 450 µl of cold isopropanol was added and then centrifuged at 13,000 rpm for 5 minutes to precipitate the DNA pellet. After precipitation the pellet was recovered, washed with 450µl of ethanol 70°C cold and then centrifuged at 12,000rpm at 4°C for 5min. After centrifugation the pellet was dried until the ethanol evaporated completely. The extracted DNA was suspended in 75 µl of TE 1X buffer and then treated with RNAase. After treatment with RNAase the DNA was stored at -20°C until use. The concentration and purity of the DNA samples was evaluated using a *NanoDrop 8000 thermofisher* (Photo 5). The quality of the extracted DNA was analysed using a 1% agarose gel.

Photo 5: Dosing with the nano-spectrophotometer

3.2.2   Choice of microsatellite primers, reaction medium and PCR amplification, electrophoresis

To identify polymorphic SSR markers, a screening was carried out using 15 pairs of primers (Table 5). The selected polymorphic markers were then used to study the diversity of our population. The reaction volume is 25µl and includes 3 µl of genomic DNA (10 ng / µl),

2.5µl of 10X buffer, 2 µl of dNTP (2.5 mM), 2µl of MgCl2 (25mM), 0.05µl of each primer, 0.2µl of 0.5U Taq polymerase and 15.2µl of ultrapure water. Amplification was performed with the SWIFT MINIPRO Prime3 thermocycler and the PCR programme used was as follows: 37 cycles including one (1) DNA pre-denaturation cycle at 95oC for 1 min followed by a set of 35 cycles with denaturation for 30s at 95oC, hybridization at 55oC for 30s and extension for 30s at 72oC. A final phase containing only a 5 min extension at 72oC. The PCR products are migrated on an agarose gel (2% gel) at 135 V for 30 min and then visualised on a documentation gel system. In order to be able to identify the sizes of the different PCR bands, a marker of 1kb size was used.

Table 5: List of the 15 primer pairs used

3.2.3   Analysis of the results

The processing of the data collected during the sampling was done using the Excel

N°	Name	Sequences	Number of bases	Tm
1	MA1-32	F: GGA-ACA-GGT-GAT-CAA-AGT-GTG-A	22	47.9°C
		R: TTG-ATC-ATG-TGC-CGC-CGC-TAC-TG	20	60.0°C
2	MA3-90	F: GCA-CGA-AGA-GGC-ATC-AC	17	54.0°C
		R: GGC-CAA-ATT-TGA-TGG-ACT	18	52.0°C
3	MMACIR01	F: TTA-AAG-GTG-GGT-TAG-CAT-TAG-G	22	46.0°C
		R: TTT-GAT-GTC-ACA-ATG-GTG-TTC-C	22	46.0°C
4	MMACIR03	F: TGA-CCC-ACG-AGA-AAA-GAA-GC	20	60.0°C
		R: CTC-CTC-CAT-AGC-CTG-ACT-GC	20	64.0°C
5	MMACIR07	F: AAC-AAC-TAG-GAT-GGT-AAT-GTG-TGG-AA	26	49.7°C
		R: GAT-CTG-AGG-ATG-GTT-CTG-TTG-GAG-TG	26	54.4°C
6	MMACIR08	F: ACT-TAT-TCC-CCC-GCA-CTC-AA	20	60.0°C
		R: ACT-CTC-GCC-CAT-CTT-CAT-CC	20	62.0°C
7	MMACIR13	F: TCC-CAA-CCC-CTG-CAA-CCA-CT	20	64.0°C
		R: ATG-ACC-TGT-CGA-ACA-TCC-TTT	21	45.3°C
8	MMACIR150	F: ATG-CTG-TCA-TTG-CCT-TGT	18	52.0°C
		R: GAA-TGC-TGA-TAC-CTC-TTT-GG	20	58.0°C
9	MMACIR152	F: CCA-CCT-TTG-AGT-TCT-CTC-C	19	58.0°C
		R: TTT-CCC-TCT-TCG-ATT-CTG-T	19	54.0°C
10	MMACIR164	F: AAG-ACA-AGT-TCC-ATT-GCT-TG	20	56.0°C
		R: GTT-CGG-GCT-TTC-GGT	15	48.0°C
11	MMACIR196	F: GCT-CCA-AAC-CTC-CCT-TT	17	52.0°C
		R: CGA-TGC-CAC-ACT-GGA-C	16	52.0°C
12	MMACIR214	F: CCA-TTG-AGA-GAT-CAA-CCC	18	54.0°C
		R: CTA-TTT-GAC-GTT-GGT-GGT-C	19	56.0°C
13	MMACIR231	F: GCA-AAT-AGT-CAA-GGG-AAT-CA	20	56.0°C
		R: ACC-CAG-GTC-TAT-CAG-GTC-A	19	58.0°C
14	MMACIR24	F: ATC-TTT-TCT-TAT-CCT-TCT-AAC-G	22	42.3°C
		R: ATT-AGA-TCA-CCG-AAG-AAC-TC	20	56.0°C
15	MMACIR260	F: GAT-GTT-TGG-GCT-GTT-TCT-T	19	54.0°C
		R: AAG-CAG-GTC-AGA-TTG-TTC-C	19	56.0°C

2013 spreadsheet. Numerical values are assigned to the bands and the resulting data is entered as an allelic composition at each locus in Excel for analysis. Version 6.502 of the GenAIEx software (Peakall and Smouse, 2012) was used to perform the genetic data analysis. The total number of alleles, allele frequency, number of alleles per locus for each locus and population, observed heterozygosity and genetic diversity (He) (Nei, 1973) were calculated. The indices of genetic dissimilarity between genotypes were calculated using DARwin 6 software (Perrier and Jacquemoud-Collet, 2006) in order to graphically represent the relationships between accessions. A principal component analysis (PCA) was also carried out in order to visualise the distribution of accessions according to their microsatellite diversity. Finally, an analysis of molecular variance (AMOVA) was also carried out using the GenAIEx software in order to estimate the total molecular variance between and within populations.

CHAPTER III: RESULTS AND DISCUSSION

1. Results

1.1 Varietal diversity of dessert and plantain bananas

A total of 59 accessions of dessert banana trees were sampled and distributed by the collection departments. Table 6 shows a wide diversity of dessert bananas in the Mono-Couffo department (42.4%) followed by the Atlantic department (35.6%) and the Zou and collines departments (22%). Figure 4 graphically illustrates the distribution of the different varieties by department.

Table 6: Varietal diversity of dessert bananas

Department	Number of varieties	Percentage
Atlantic	21	35,6
Mono-Couffo	25	42,4
Zou-Collines	13	22

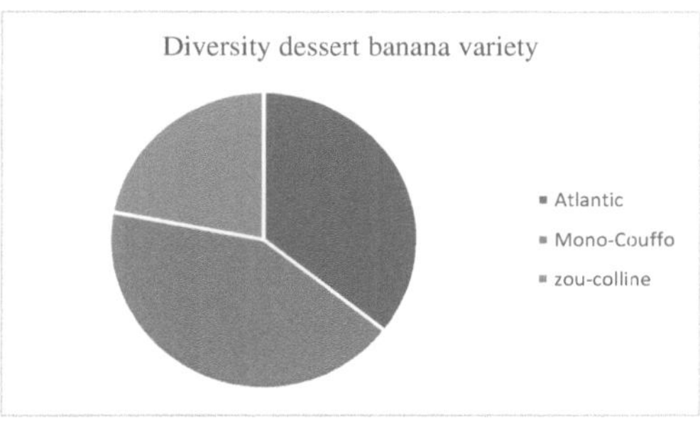

Figure 4*: Varietal diversity of dessert bananas*

The distribution of the 35 accessions of plantain bananas per collection department (Table 7) shows us a great varietal diversity in the Mono-Couffo department (57.1%) followed by the Atlantic department (22.9%) and the Zou-Collines department (20%). The different distributions are shown graphically in Figure 5.

<u>**Table 7**</u>: Varietal diversity of Plantain bananas

Department	Number of varieties	Percentage
Atlantic	8	22,9
Mono-Couffo	20	57,1
Zou-Collines	7	20

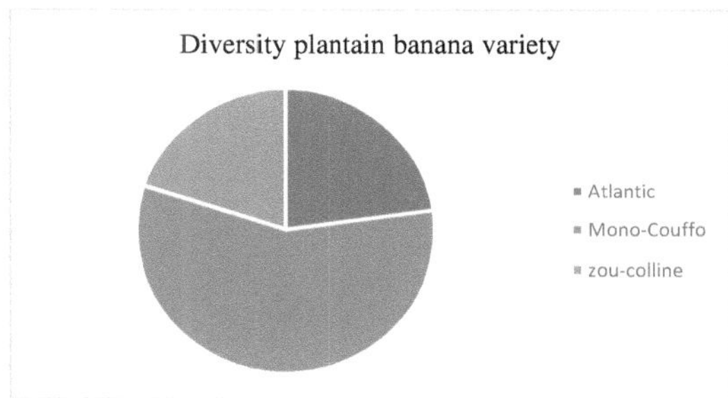

Figure 5*: Varietal diversity of plantain bananas*

1.2 Selection of polymorphic markers

Of the 15 microsatellite markers identified, seven (6) amplified in plantain, including 2 polymorphs. For dessert bananas, 7 markers amplified out of the 15, including 4 polymorphs. Table 8 summarises the markers used on each variety and their mono/polymorphic characteristics. As shown in the photo of the gel after migration (Photo 6), a variation in the number of bands per sample can be observed and heterozygosity and homozygosity are also highlighted.

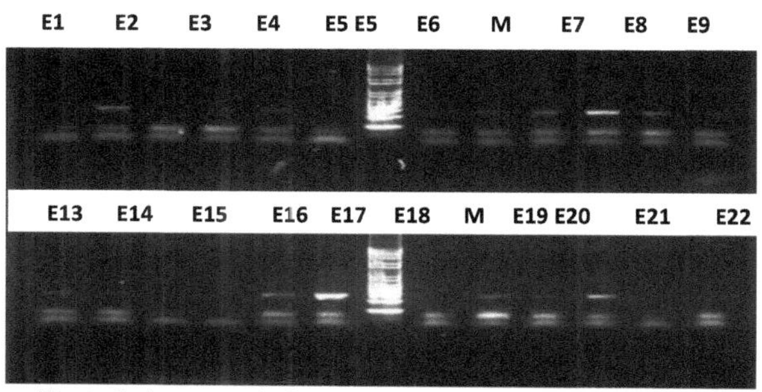

<u>**Photo 6**</u>: Agarose gel after migration. **M=** weight marker; **E=** sample

<u>**Table 8**</u>: List of the primers identified for the diversity study

SRG SSR	Polymorhpism	Varieties	Band size
MA1-32	YES	Dessert	100-210
MMACIR01	YES	Plantain	185-410
MMACIR08	YES	Dessert	150-175
MMACIR150	YES	Dessert	130-240
MMACIR152	YES	Plantain	152-480
MMACIR214	YES	Dessert	150-420

1.3 Analysis of the genetic diversity of plantains

1.3.1   Identification and Polymorphism of the microsatellite markers used

Out of a total of fifteen (15) primers tested, two (2) presented an exploitable polymorphism (83.33%) for the diversity study. This represents a rate of 13.33%. Based on the two pairs of polymorphic primers previously identified, a diversity analysis was carried out on our study population. The number of alleles produced by each primer varies from 2 to 4. The lowest number of alleles is observed with the **MMACIR01** locus and the highest number of alleles is obtained with the **MMACIR152** locus (Table 9). A total of 6 alleles were obtained for the two primer pairs used. Table 9 summarizes the information relating to the 2 microsatellite loci and the 6 corresponding alleles. The allelic frequencies vary from 0 to 1 within the populations for the different loci considered and are shown in Figure 6. Two private alleles of sizes 450 and 480 respectively were detected.

<u>**Table 9**</u>: Summary of the number of alleles by locus

Alleles	MMACIR01	MMACIR152
185	1	1
250	0	1
410	1	0
450	0	1
480	0	1
Total No. Alleles	2	4

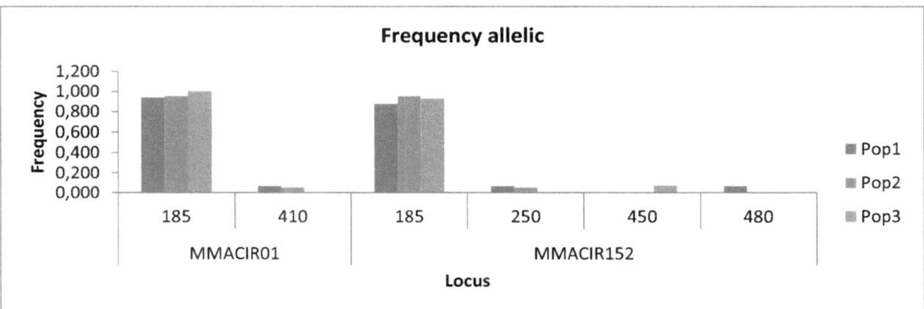

Figure 6*: Representative diagram of the variation in allelic frequencies by locus within the populations studied. Pop1= Atlantic; Pop2= Mono-Couffo; Pop3= Zou-Collines*

1.3.2 Diversity parameters of the microsatellite loci used

Table 10 groups together the parameters of genetic diversity determined : Na (mean number of different alleles), Ne (mean effective number of alleles), I (Shannon diversity index), Ho (observed heterozygosity), He (expected heterozygosity), and F or Fis (binding index). Genetic diversity ranged from 0.144±0.073 to 0.306±0.080 with a mean of 0.225±C.061. The observed heterozygosity varied from 0.071±0.036 to 0.151±0.039 with a mean of 0.111±0.030. The lowest value was obtained with the MMACIR01 locus and the highest with the MMACIR152 locus. The fixation index F, presents values that vary between -0.060±0.006 and -0.078±0.015 with an average of 0.070±0.009 (Table 10).

Table 10: Diversity parameters of different microsatellite loci

	MMACIR01	MMACIR152	Average
N	11.667±4.177	11.667±4.177	11.667±2.642
Na	1.667±0.333	2.333±0.333	2.000±0.258
Do	1.079±0.040	1.184±0.056	1.131±0.039
I	0.144±0.073	0.306±0.080	0.225±0.061
Ho	0.075±0.038	0.164±0.045	0.120±0.033
He	0.071±0.036	0.151±0.039	0.111±0.030
F	-0.060±0.006	-0.078±0.015	-0.070±0.009

N: Effective number of individuals, Na: Average number of different alleles, Ne: Average effective number of alleles,
I: Shannon diversity index, Ho: Observed heterozygosity, He: Expected heterozygosity (genetic diversity)
F : Fixing index

1.3.3 Genetic variability in the population

The analysis of heterozygosity across the different collection sites showed a very low level of diversity in all populations with respective values of 0.172; 0.095, and 0.066 for the Atlantic, Mono-Couffo and Zou-Collines populations. The lowest heterozygosity (He = 0.066) was observed for the Zou-Collines banana population (Table 11). As for the index of genetic diversity, the lowest value was always observed at the Zou-Collines population level and confirms the status of the low level of diversity in this region (Table 11). Analysis of genetic differentiation (Table 11) based on genetic distances shows that the lowest genetic differentiation is observed between the Atlantic and Mono-Couffo populations, while the highest is between the Atlantic and Zou-Collines populations.

Table 11: Variability in the diversity of parameters across regions

Population	Atlantic	Mono-Couffo	Zou-Collines
Na	2.500±0.5	2.000	1.500±0.5
Do	1.213±0.080	1.105	1.076±0.076
I	0.349±0.115	0.199	0.129±0.129
Unique Allele	0.500±0.5	0.000	0.500±0.5
He	0.172	0.095	0.066

<u>**Table 12**</u>: Matrix of genetic differentiation between populations

Region	Atlantic	Mono-Couffo	Zou-Collines
Atlantic	0.000		
Mono-Couffo	0.008	0.000	
Zou-Collines	0.027	0.022	0.000

1.3.4   Genetic Structuring and Molecular Variance Analysis

In order to be able to highlight intra- and inter-population variations, an analysis of molecular variance (AMOVA) was carried out and the results are recorded in Table 13. The results showed that variation can only be defined at the individual level. No variability is observed at the intra- and inter-population level.

<u>**Table 13**</u>: Analysis of Molecular Variance (AMOVA)

Source	df	SS	MS	East. Var.	%
Between population	2	0.136	0.068	0.000	0%
Within the populations	32	3.479	0.109	0.000	0%
Within individuals	35	4.000	0.114	0.114	100%
Total	69	7.614		0.114	100%

The dissimilarity matrix generated made it possible to realise phylogenetic relationships between individuals in the form of phylogenetic trees. Figure 7 shows the resulting phylogenetic tree. Three blocks can be distinguished of which block 1 consists of 30 individuals, block 2 consists of 3 individuals and block 3 consists of 2 individuals (Figure 7). The individuals in block 1 come from the Atlantic, Mono-Couffo and Zou-Collines regions, those in block 2 from the Atlantic and Mono-Couffo regions and those in block 3 from the Atlantic and Zou-Collines regions.

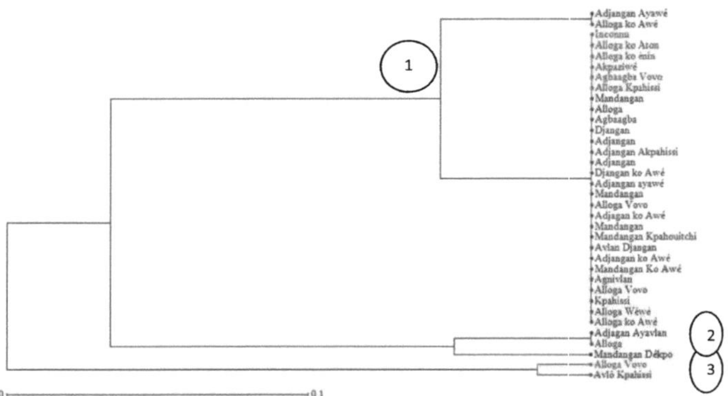

__Figure 7__: Dendrogram grouping the different individuals according to their genetic similarity. Red=Altlantic; Blue= Mono-Couffo; Green= Zou-Collines

1.4 Analysis of the genetic diversity of dessert bananas

1.4.1   Polymorphism of the microsatellite markers used

Of the 15 primer pairs tested, only four showed a rate of polymorphism that could be used for the diversity study. This represents a rate of 26.66%. Table 14 shows the rate of polymorphism and the frequencies of the different alleles. Moreover, the rate of polymorphism within the populations varies from 47.37% to 68.42% with an average of 61.40%. The Atlantic(1) and Mono-Couffo(2) populations show the highest and identical rates, while the lowest rate is observed in the Zou-Collines(3) population. The number of alleles per population is 14, 15, 11 for populations 1, 2 and 3 respectively. The number of private alleles also varies within the populations. It is 2, 3, 1 for populations 1, 2 and 3 respectively.

Table 14: Polymorphism rate and allele frequency

	Atlantic	Mono-Couffo	Zou-Collines
Rate of polymorphism of loci per population	68.42%	68.42%	47.37%
Average polymorphism		61.40 ± 7.02	
Number of alleles	14	15	11
Number of alleles with frequency >= 5%.	9	10	11
Number of private alleles	2	3	1

1.4.2   Genetic variability in the population

Table 15 presents the parameters of diversity within the different populations. The average number of different alleles ranges from 1,053 to 1,474 with an average of 1,316 ± 0,120. The Shannon diversity index varies from 0.212 to 0.234 with an average of 0.220. As for the heterozygosity rate, it varies from 0.128 to 0.155 with an average of 0.137, reflecting the very low genetic diversity within the different populations studied.

Table 15: Parameters of diversity within populations

	N	Na	Do	I	He
Atlantic	21.000	1.421±0.207	1.179±0.052	0.213±0.049	0.126±0.033
Mono-Couffo	25.000	1.474±0.193	1.193±0.062	0.212±0.052	0.128±0.036
Zou-Collines	13.000	1.053±0.223	1.266±0.085	0.234±0.065	0.155±0.046
Average	19.667±0.667	1.316±0.120	1.213±0.039	0.220±0.032	0.137±0.022

Analysis of genetic differentiation (Table 16) based on genetic distances also showed that the lowest genetic differentiation was observed between the Atlantic and Mono-Couffo populations, while the highest genetic differentiation was between the Atlantic and Zou-Collines populations. However, the level of differentiation observed remains extremely low. These values reflect a low level of genetic differentiation between populations.

Table 16: Matrix of genetic differentiation between different populations

Populations	Atlantic	Mono-Couffo	Zou-Collines
Atlantic	0.000		
Mono-Couffo	0.192	0.000	
Zou-Collines	0.246	0.242	0.000

In order to highlight intra- and inter-population variations, a molecular analysis of variance (AMOVA) was carried out and the results are recorded in the following table. The results showed that variability can be defined at two levels, at the interpopulation and intrapopulation levels. However, this genetic variability is much more marked at the intrapopulation level with a rate of 78%.

Table 17: Analysis of Molecular Variance (AMOVA)

	df	SS	MS	East. Var.	%
Interpopulation	2	22.118	11.059	0.490	22%
Intrapopulation	56	97.068	1.733	1.733	78%
Total	58	119.186		2.223	100%

1.4.3   Genetic Structuring and Principal Component Analysis

In order to better visualise the distribution of the different individuals, a projection based on genetic distances was made in the plane along two axes (Figure 8). The first two axes (axis 1 and axis 2) of the PCA show respectively percentages of inertia of 32.91% and 14.43% with a cumulative value of 47.34%. The distribution observed shows that there is no structuring between the different populations.

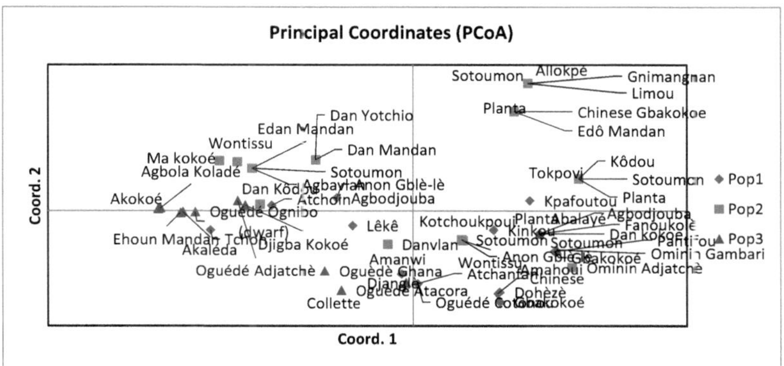

Figure 8*: Main Component Analysis*

Similarly, the dissimilarity matrix generated has made it possible to create phylogenetic relationships between individuals in the form of a phylogenetic tree. The figure below shows the phylogenetic tree thus obtained. Three blocks can be distinguished, including blocks 1 and 2 made up of individuals from the three populations, and block 3 comprising 2 individuals from the Atlantic and the Zou-Collines.

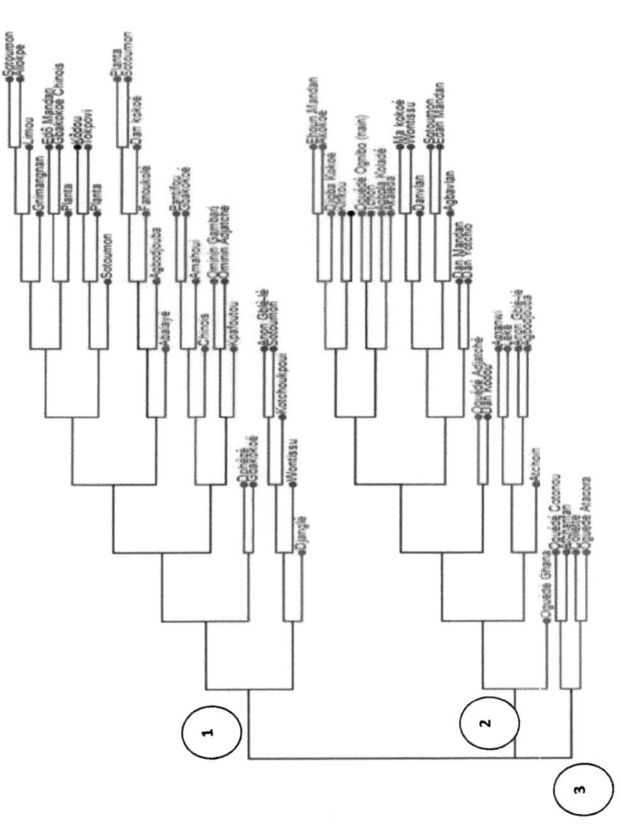

Figure 9: *Dendrogram grouping the different individuals according to their genetic similarity. Red= Atlantic; Green= Zou-Collines; Blue= Mono-Couffo*

2. Discussion

Knowledge of the level of diversity of cultivated bananas is a prerequisite for any programme to improve, conserve and manage its genetic resources. Moreover, the application of molecular markers is an essential element in determining the existing level of diversity. Indeed, according to the work of Pedro et al (1999) and Adéoti et al (2016), there is a great diversity of cultivated banana trees in Benin based on the vernacular names assigned. Subject to homonymy and synonymy, 75 vernacular names were listed by Adeoti et al. (2016) corresponding to dessert and plantain bananas. A small number of microatellite markers made it possible to study the diversity, out of 15 markers, 6 were amplified, including 2 polymorphs. With a polymorphism rate of 13.33% observed for the microsatellite markers applied to plantain bananas, the mean heterozygosity is 0.111 ± 0.030, the number of alleles obtained per locus being 3 against 2.5 obtained by Noyer et al.(2005). This reflects on the one hand a very low polymorphism of the markers used, and on the other hand a low level of diversity within the plantain bananas studied. The markers used were reported to be extremely polymorphic on banana trees. However, the low level of polymorphism observed could result from the fact that a small portion of the genome is covered by these markers. Indeed, the work of Noyer et al (2005) had shown a low level of polymorphism in plantains using polymorphic markers described by Grapin et al (1998). Furthermore, the use of the same markers by Creste et al. (2003) on different varieties did not allow differentiation between them given the very low level of polymorphism observed. Furthermore, Crouch et al. (1998; 199a; 1999b) reported in their study on the genetic diversity of banana trees using microsatellite markers that the lack of amplification at the level of certain genotypes could be linked to the variation of flanking sequences on microsatellite loci at the level of the banana genome, which would lead to the observation of null alleles or a reduction in amplification. This could introduce biases in the determination of genetic distances and differentiation coefficients. The differentiation observed between the plantain populations in our study remains very low and the reduced number of polymorphic markers used could also contribute to this. Although the regions are remote, there is almost no difference between populations. These results probably show that the genetic base of plantains would be reduced. The construction of the phylogenetic tree obtained on the basis of genetic distances showed three genetic groups 1, 2, 3 composed of 30, 3 and 2 accessions respectively. Group 1 is very heterogeneous comprising both individuals from the 3 different regions. As the vernacular names may vary from one ethnic group to another and from one region to another, based on the groupings obtained, it follows that the accessions named Alloga, adjangan, Mandangan, Agbaagba, Akoziwé, Alloga kô awé, would designate the same variety.

The reproduction of banana trees being almost exclusively by vegetative propagation, and the way in which the varieties are acquired by the producers, i.e. exchange or purchase, have factors that could justify the fact that the same varieties are found in different regions under different names. These results partly confirm the information collected in the field from producers and clarify the aspect of synonymies and homonymy of names observed in the varieties collected. The varieties Alloga ako awé and Adjangan akpaziwé both designate the same variety. Only the varieties Avlô kpahissi and Alloga vôvô would clearly indicate varieties that are different from the molecular point of view of all the other varieties in the Atlantic and Zou-Collines departments respectively. Indeed, the only private alleles were observed in these two varieties. As for dessert bananas, the rate of polymorphism observed at the loci was 61.40%. This rate is lower than those observed by Amorin et al (2012) and Irish et al (2014). This difference could be related to the low number of microsatellite markers used and the sample size compared to previous studies. The observed heterozygosity reflecting the level of diversity is 0.137 and indicates a very low level of diversity within the studied populations. This value is lower than those reported by Amorin et al (2012) and Irish et al (2014) which are 0.6526 and 0.81 respectively. Molecule analysis of variance coupled with the determination of genetic differentiation revealed a low level of differentiation between populations. Moreover, the maximum differentiation, i.e. 78%, was observed at the intra-population level. This could justify the large number of varieties found within a given region, i.e. 7, 11 and 13 respectively for Mono-Couffo, Atlantic and Zou-Collines. The principal component analysis did not make it possible to group accessions on the basis of their belonging to different departments. However, the phylogenetic tree obtained made it possible to group the different accessions of the populations on the basis of their genetic dissimilarity into three large distinct groups. Indeed all the groups are heterogeneous and include both varieties different from the three regions or varieties with the same name but from different regions. Indeed, the "sotoumon" variety is found both in groups 1 and 2 on the one hand and at different levels of the tree within group 1 on the other. This could be due to the fact that they are genetically different varieties. This was the case with plantain bananas in the past.

CONCLUSION AND OUTLOOK

Microsatellite markers have proved to be very useful in the study of banana tree diversity. In view of the results obtained, genetic diversity remains low in both the dessert bananas and the plantains studied. No genetic structuring according to zones was observed within the two types of bananas. In fact, on the basis of the dendrogram obtained for the plantain bananas, several vernacular names supposedly designating different varieties were found to designate the same variety. In the case of dessert bananas, the diversity of vernacular names observed also translates in the majority of cases as genetically different varieties. In addition, particular or private alleles could be observed in dessert and plantain bananas. Two private alleles were observed in plantain and five in dessert bananas. These results are preliminary and deserve to be further investigated through future studies.

The research perspectives arising from this diversity study on banana varieties grown in Benin will have to be oriented in the direction of :

- The use of a larger number of polymorphic microsatellite markers
- The agromorphological characterisation of the studied varieties
- A combined analysis of agromorphological and molecular data for a better characterization of the varieties, and
- Determining the ploidy level of banana varieties

BIBLIOGRAPHICAL REFERENCES

BIBLIOGRAPHICAL REFERENCES

ADEOTI K., G. DJEDATIN, E. EWEDJE, A. AFFOKPON, M. FAÏNOU, F. TOUKOUROU,

2016. Collection, characterisation and evaluation of banana varieties grown in Benin. Report 1st year. 19p

Adéoti, Kifouli, DJEDATIN Gustave, EWEDJE Ebenezer, BEULE Thierry, SANTONI Sylvain, RIVAL Alain, JALIGOT Estelle, 2017. "Assessment of Genetic Diversity among Cultivated Pearl Millet (Pennisetum Glaucum, Poaceae) Accessions from Benin, West Africa." *African Journal of Biotechnology* 16 (15):782-90.

Agre, Sourou, 2015. "Genetic Diversity and Evaluation of the Agronomic Performance of Elite Manioc (Manihot Esculenta Crantz) Cultivars Grown in Benin"75p

Akinbo, Olalekan Abiodun. 2008. "Introgression of High Protein and Pest Resistance Genes from Inter-Specific Hybrids of Manihot Esculenta Ssp Flabellifolia into Cassava (Manihot Esculenta Crantz)," 12p

BAKRY, Frédéric, CARREEL Françoise, CARUANA Marie-Line, Côte François-Xavier, JENNY Christophe, TEZENAS Du Montcel Hugues. 2002. "Les Bananiers." 109–131.

Castelblanco, W, M. Fregene. 2006. "SSCP-SNP-Based Conserved Ortholog Set (COS) Markers for Comparative Genomics in Cassava (Manihot Esculenta Crantz)." *Plant Molecular Biology Reporter* 24 (2):229-236.

Champion, J. 1963. *The Banana Tree*. G-P House. Paris.263p

Dettori, Maria Teresa, Roberta Quarta, Ignazio Verde. 2001. "A Peach Linkage Map Integrating RFLPs, SSRs, RAPDs, and Morphological Markers." *Genome* 44 (5):783-90.

Doležel, Jaroslav, Jan Bartoš. 2005. "Plant DNA Flow Cytometry and Estimation of Nuclear Genome Size." *Annals of Botany* 95 (1):99-110.

Doré, C., and F. Varoquaux. 2006. *History and Improvement of Fifty Cultivated Plants*. Know-how. Paris, France. 812p

Ellis, T H N. 1994. "Approaches to the Genetic Mapping of Pea." In *Vegetables and Vegetable Products*, edited by Hans Ferdinand Linskens and John F Jackson, 117-160.

Fregene, M A, M Suarez, J Mkumbira, H Kulembeka, E Ndedya, A Kulaya, S Mitchel, . 2003. "Simple Sequence Repeat Marker Diversity in Cassava Landraces: Genetic Diversity and Differentiation in an Asexually Propagated Crop." *Theoretical and Applied Genetics* 107 (6):1083-1093.

Ganry, Jacky, Eric Fouré, Luc de Laperye de Bellaire, Thierry Lescot. 2012. "An Integrated Approach to Control the Black Leaf Streak Disease (BLSD) of Bananas, While Reducing Fungicide Use and Environmental Impact." In *Fungicides for Plant and Animal Diseases*, edited by A. Dhanasekaran, D.; Thajuddin, N.; Panneerselvam, 193-226.

Gbahoun, Alphonse. 1993. "Savoir Pour Mieux Vulgariser et Mieux Cultiver : Les Principales Cultures Du Bénin," 178p.

Gupta, P. K., S. Rustgi. 2004. "Molecular Markers from the Transcribed/expressed Region of the Genome in Higher Plants." *Functional and Integrative Genomics* 4 (3):139-62.

INFOCOMM, UN. 2016. "CAFE - A Commodity Profile By INFOCOMM," 42p.

Irish, Brian M., Hugo E. Cuevas, Sheron a. Simpson, Brian E. Scheffler, Julie Sardos, Randy Ploetz, Ricardo Goenaga. 2014. "Musa Spp. Germplasm Management: Microsatellite Fingerprinting of USDA-ARS National Plant Germplasm System Collection." *Crop Science* 54 (5):2140-2151.

Jones, David. 2000. *Introduction to Banana, Abaca and Enset. Diseases of Banana, Abaca and Enset*. llll.

Langhe, E. De. 1961. "The Taxonomy of the Plantain Banana Tree in Equatorial Africa." *Journal of Tropical Agriculture and Applied Botany* 8 (10):417-449.

Lassois, Ludivine, Jean-Pièrre Busogoro, Haissam Jijakli. 2009. "La Banane: De Son Origine À Sa Commercialisation." *Biotechnology, Agronomy and Society and Environment* 13 (4):575-86.

Lassoudière, André. 2010. *The History of the Banana Tree*. Edition QU. Versailles Cedex, France.

Lasssoudière, André. 2007. *Le Bananier et Sa Culture*. Editions Q. Versailles, France. 352p

Liu, B H. 1998. *Statistical Genomics: Linkage, Mapping, and QTL Analysis*. Boca Raton, USA: CRC Press.

Lokko, Y., E Y Danquah, S K Offei, A G O Dixon, M A Gedil. 2005. "Molecular Markers Associated with a New Source of Resistance to the Cassava Mosaic Disease." *African Journal of Biotechnology* 4 (9):873-881.

Lokossou, Bernadin, and Enoch Achigan. 2000. "Bananiers Et Bananiers Plantains Notes ,

Documents And Actual Works On Banana And Plantain Trees In Benin" 1-19.

Odah, K, M Aziadekey, K Tozo, S Akpavi, R Koukouma, A Guelly, K K Kokou, 2013. "La Diversité Génétique Des Bananiers Plantains Cultivés Dans La Zone Ouest de La Région Des Plateaux Au Togo" *International journal of biological and chemical sciences* 7 (October):1910-1918.

Okogbenin, E, M Fregene. 2003. "Genetic Mapping of QTLs Affecting Productivity and Plant Architecture in a Full-Sib Cross from Non-Inbred Parents in Cassava (Manihot Esculenta Crantz)." *Theoretical and Applied Genetics* 107 (8):1452-1462.

Okogbenin, E, J Marin, M Fregene. 2008. "QTL Analysis for Early Yield in a Pseudo F2 Population of Cassava." *African Journal of Biotechnology* 7 (2):131-138.

Pédro, J. 1999. "La Production Bananière Au Bénin. 32p.

Perrier, X., H. tezenas du Montcel. 1990. "Musaid: A Computerized Determination System. " In *Identification of Genetic Diversity in the Genus Musa, Los Banos (PHL)*, edited by R. Jarret, 76-91. Montpellier (FRA): INIBAP.

Simmonds, N. W. 1956. "Botanical Results of the Banana Collecting Expedition, 1954-1955" 11 (3):463-89.

Simmonds, N W, K Shepherd. 1955. "The Taxonomy and Origins of the Cultivated Bananas." *Journal of the Linnean Society of London, Botany* 55 (359):302-312.

Simone, from SOUZA. 1988. "Plant Names in Benin's National Languages". *Flore Du Bénin*, no. Tome 3:334-407.

Singh, Wahengbam R, Singh Sorokhaibam, Karuna Shrivastava. 2014. "Analysis of Banana Genome Groups of Wild and Cultivated Cultivars of Manipur , India Using sScore Card Method." *Advances in Applied Science Research* 5 (1):35-38.

Sivirihauma, Charles. 2013. "Caractérisation Morphologique et Diversité Variétale Des Bananiers et Bananiers Plantains Dans La Province Du Nord Kivu et Le District de l'Ituri, Province Orientale, En RDC "."

Sørensen, Kirsten Kørup, Hanne Grethe Kirk, Kerstin Olsson, Rodrigo Labouriau, Jørgen Christiansen. 2008. "A Major QTL and an SSR Marker Associated with Glycoalkaloid Content in Potato Tubers from Solanum Tuberosum S. Sparsipilum Located on

Chromosome I." *Theoretical and Applied Genetics* 117 (1):111-119.

Swennen, R. 1990. "Limits of Morphotaxonomy. Names and Synonyms of Plantains in Africa and Elsewhere." In *The Identification of Genetic Diversity in the Genus Musa. Proceeding of an International Workshop*, 5-10.

Swennen, R. D. Vuylsteke. 2001. "Bananier." In *Agriculture En Afrique Tropicale*, edited by In Raekemaekers R.H.eds, 611-630.

Tanksley, S D. 1994. "Tomato Molecular Map." In *DNA-Based Markers in Plants*, edited by Ronald L Phillips and Indra K Vasil, 310-326.

Tossou, Christophe Cocou, Anne B. Floquet, Brice A. Sinsin. 2012. "Relationship between the Production and Consumption of Fruits Grown on the Allada Plateau in Southern Benin". *Fruits* 67 (1):3-12.

Weber, J L, P E May. 1989. "Abundant Class of Human DNA Polymorphisms Which Can Be Typed Using the Polymerase Chain Reaction." *American Journal of Human Genetics* 44 (3):388-396.

Xia, Ling, Kaiman Peng, Shiying Yang, Peter Wenzl, M de Vicente, Martin Fregene, Andrzej Kilian. 2005. "DArT for High-Throughput Genotyping of Cassava (Manihot Esculenta) and Its Wild Relatives." *TAG. Theoretical and Applied Genetics. Theoretische Und Angewandte Genetik* 110:1092-98.

Yan, Z, C Denneboom, A Hattendorf, O Dolstra, T Debener, P Stam, P B Visser. 2005. "Construction of an Integrated Map of Rose with AFLP, SSR, PK, RGA, RFLP, SCAR and Morphological Markers." *Theoretical and Applied Genetics* 110 (4):766-77. https://doi.org/10.1007/s00122-004-1903-6.

ANNEXES

Gel viewing system

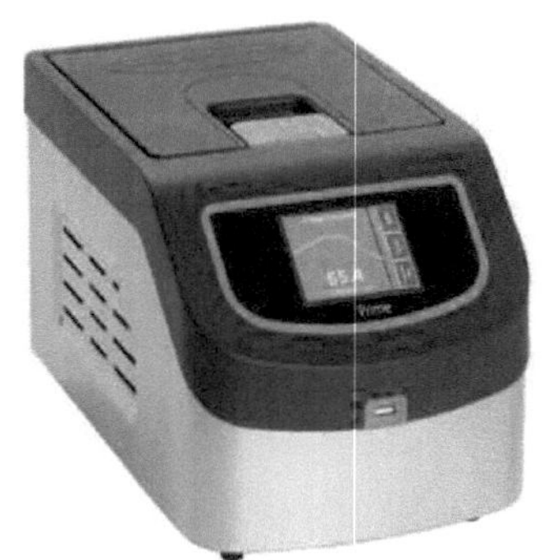

Thermocycling

Marie Bath

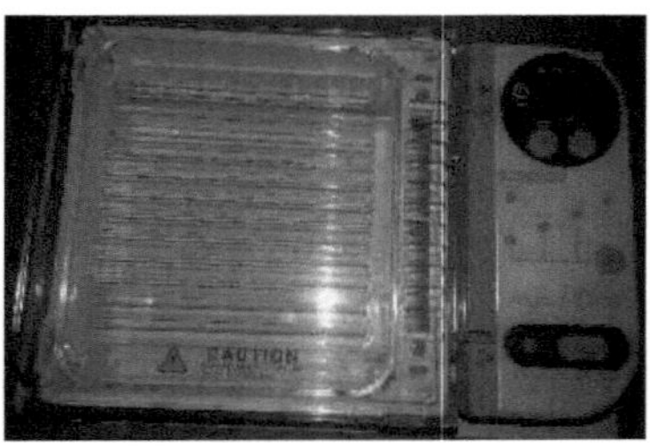

Migration Boat

Vortex

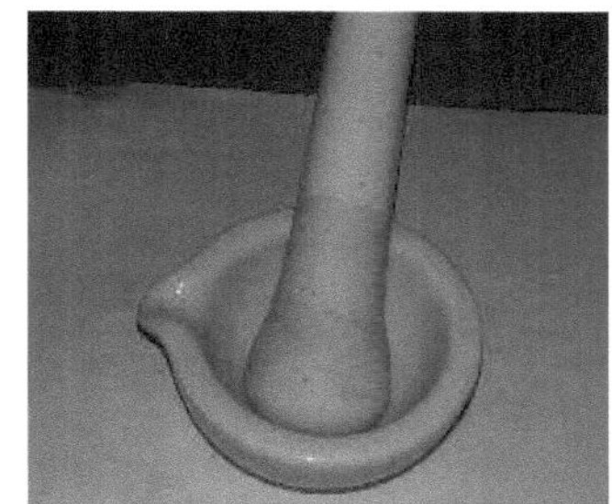

Mortar

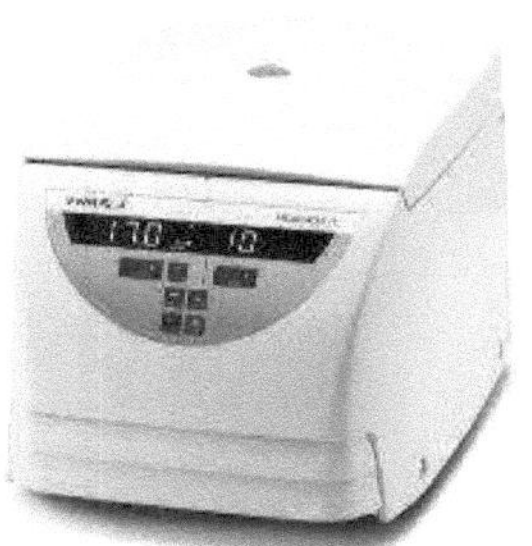

Centrifuge

TABLE OF CONTENTS

I want morebooks!

Buy your books fast and straightforward online - at one of world's fastest growing online book stores! Environmentally sound due to Print-on-Demand technologies.

Buy your books online at
www.morebooks.shop

Kaufen Sie Ihre Bücher schnell und unkompliziert online – auf einer der am schnellsten wachsenden Buchhandelsplattformen weltweit! Dank Print-On-Demand umwelt- und ressourcenschonend produziert.

Bücher schneller online kaufen
www.morebooks.shop

KS OmniScriptum Publishing
Brivibas gatve 197
LV-1039 Riga, Latvia
Telefax: +371 686 204 55

info@omniscriptum.com
www.omniscriptum.com